Cute Fashion

Coloring Book for Girls

SMALL BUTTERFLY

Printed in The U.S.A.

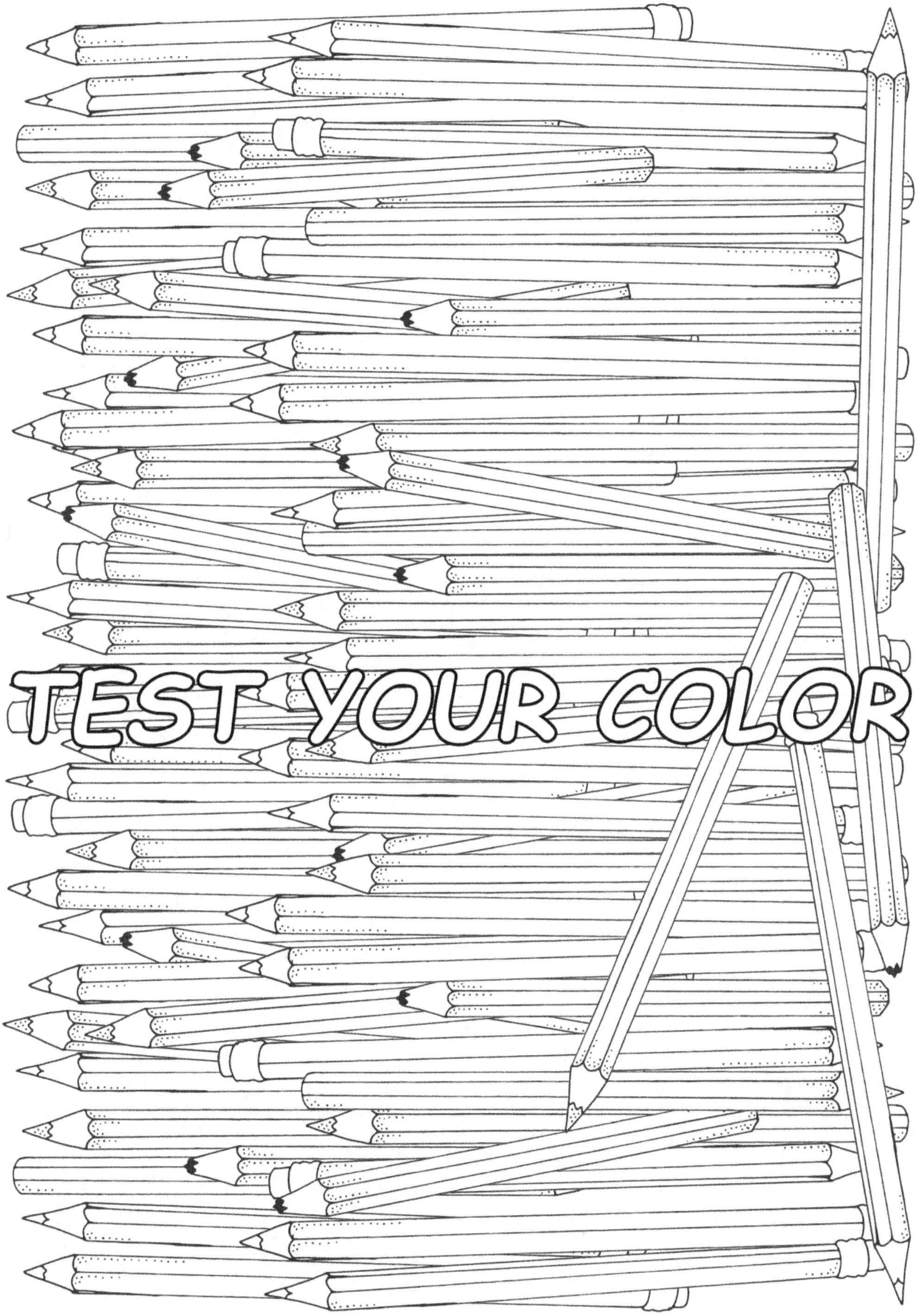
TEST YOUR COLOR

1.

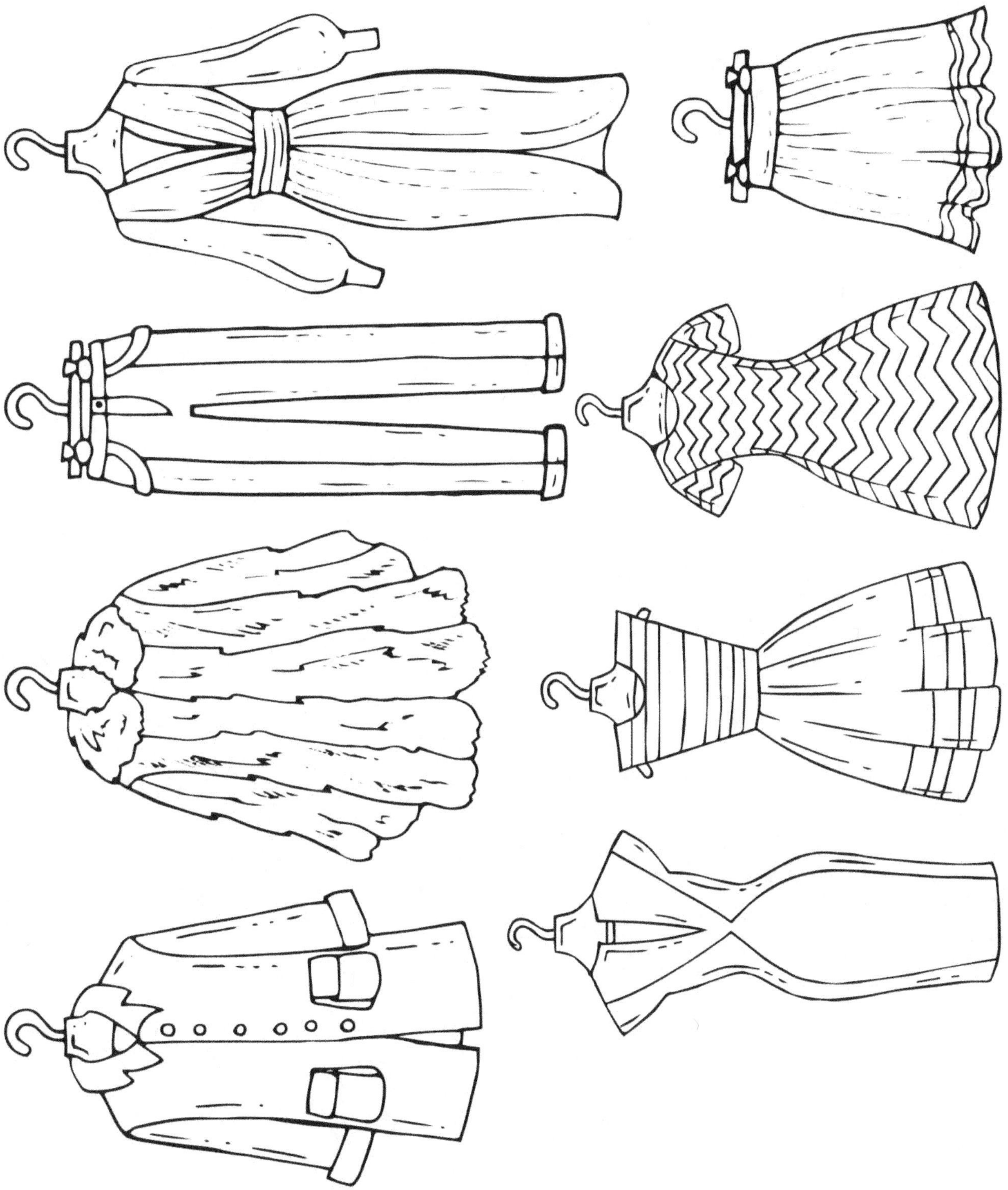

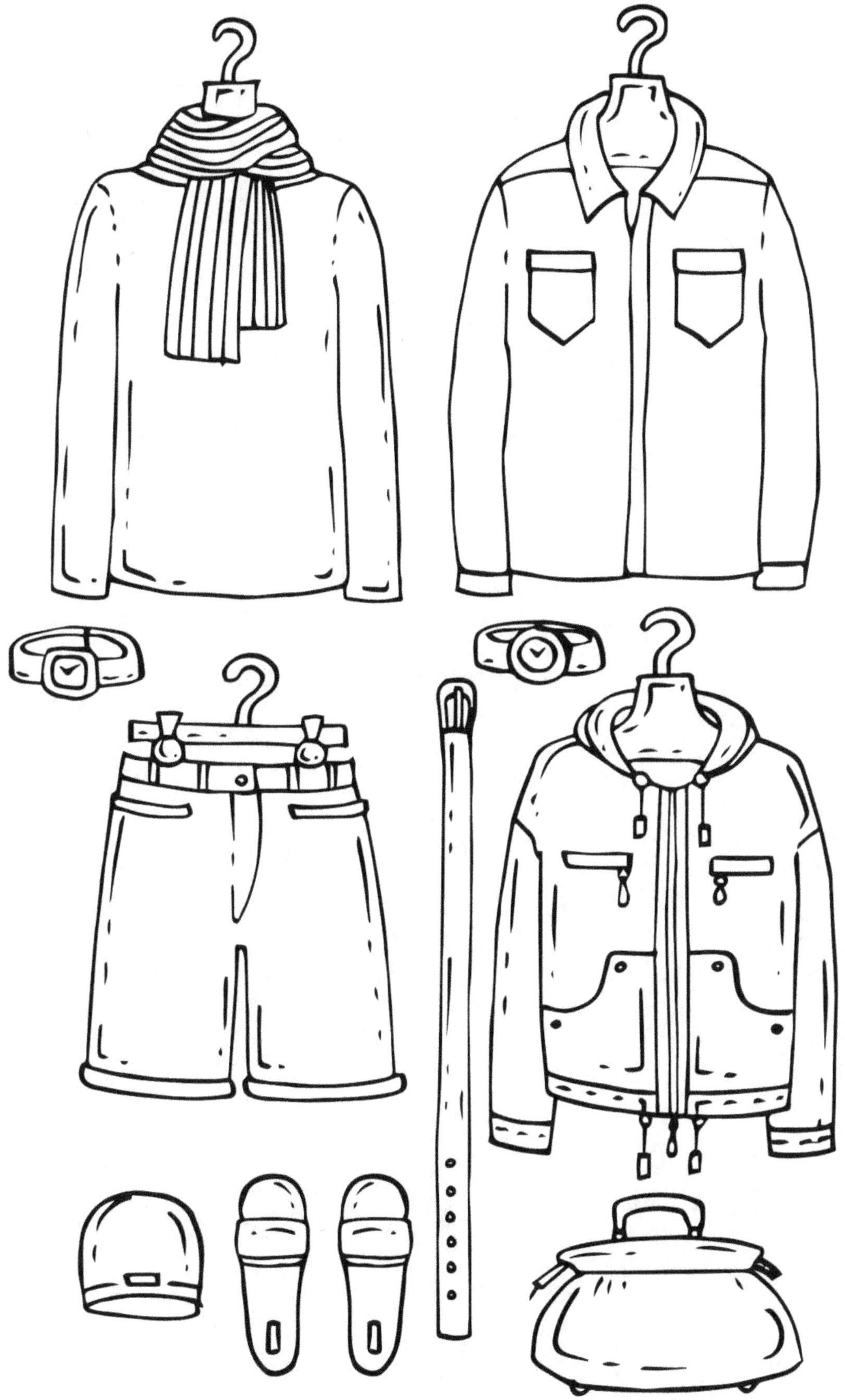

Wedding Day

SUPPER CAT
We 'RE SaFE

Wedding Day
Mr and Mrs

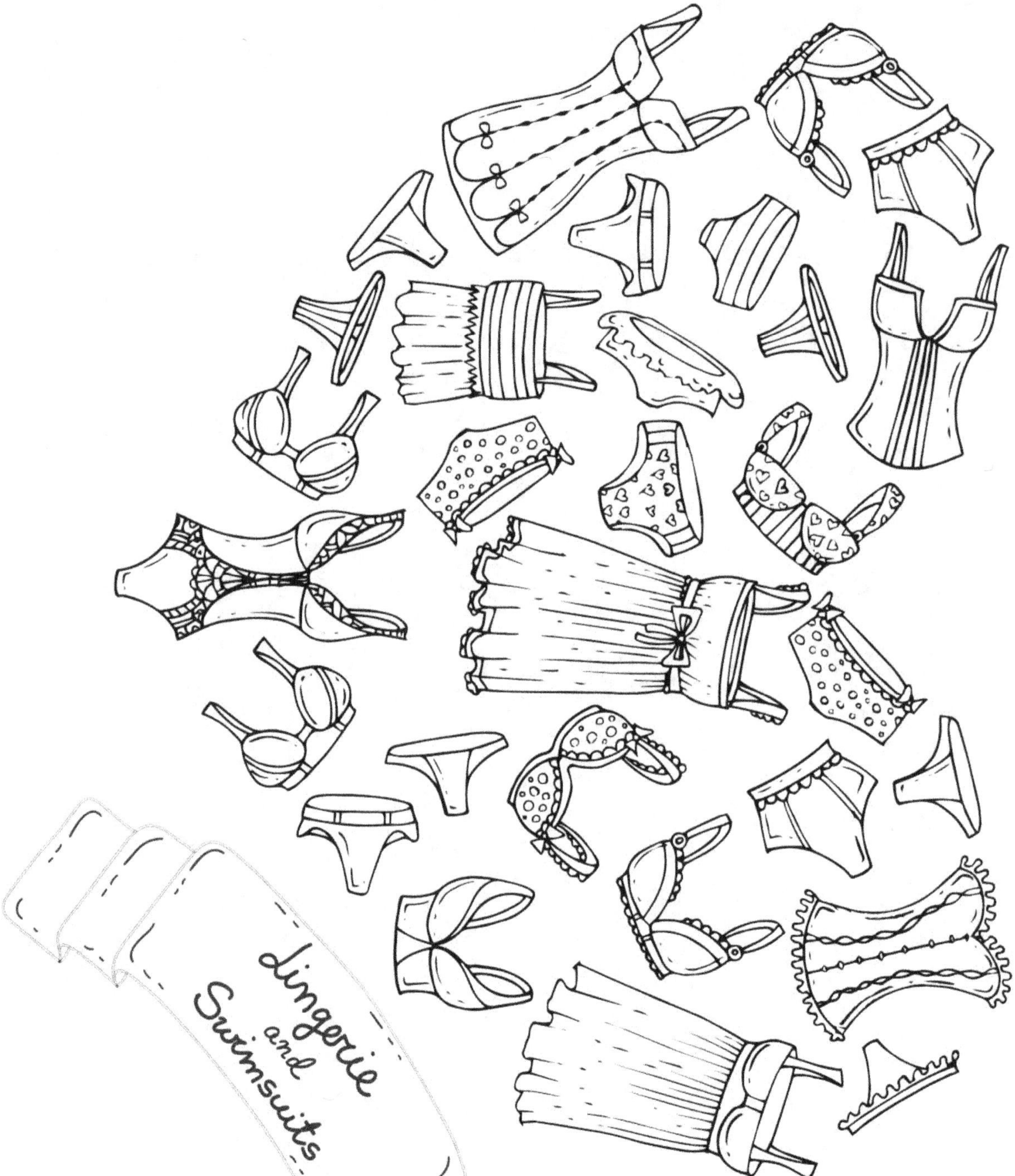
Lingerie
and
Swimsuits

Lingerie and Swimsuits

Lingerie

Lingerie
and
Swimsuits

SUPPER CAT
We 'RE SaFE

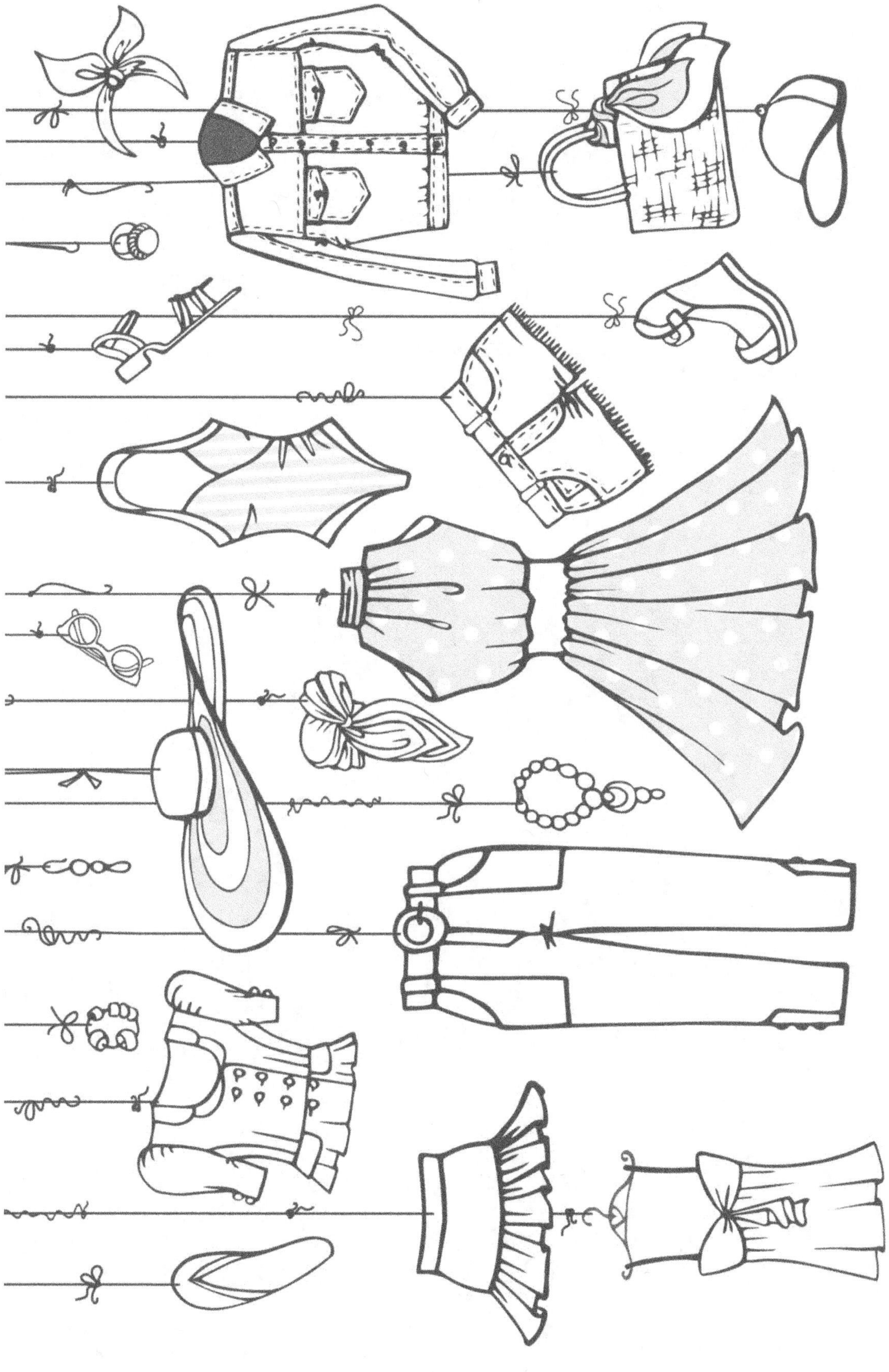

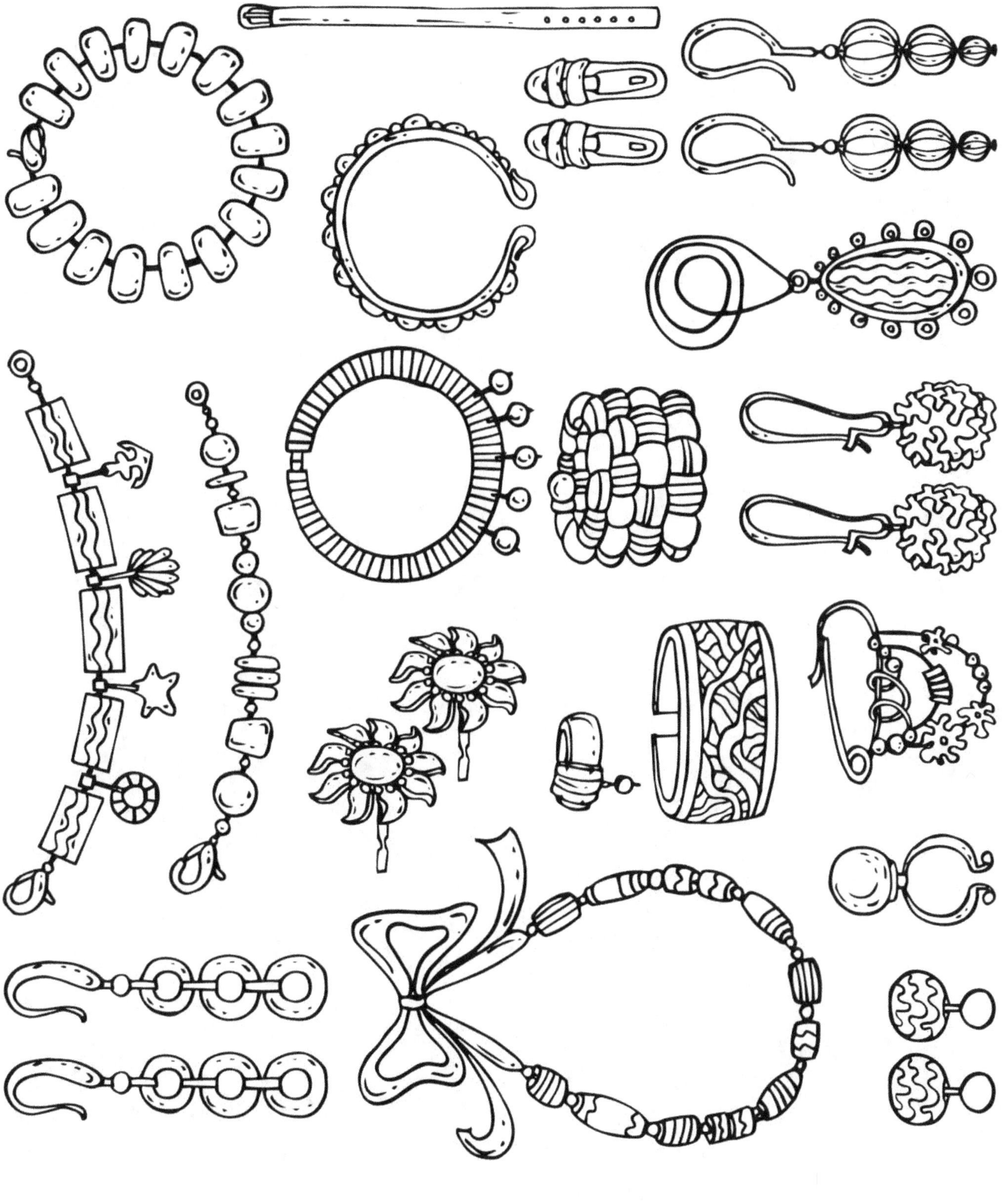

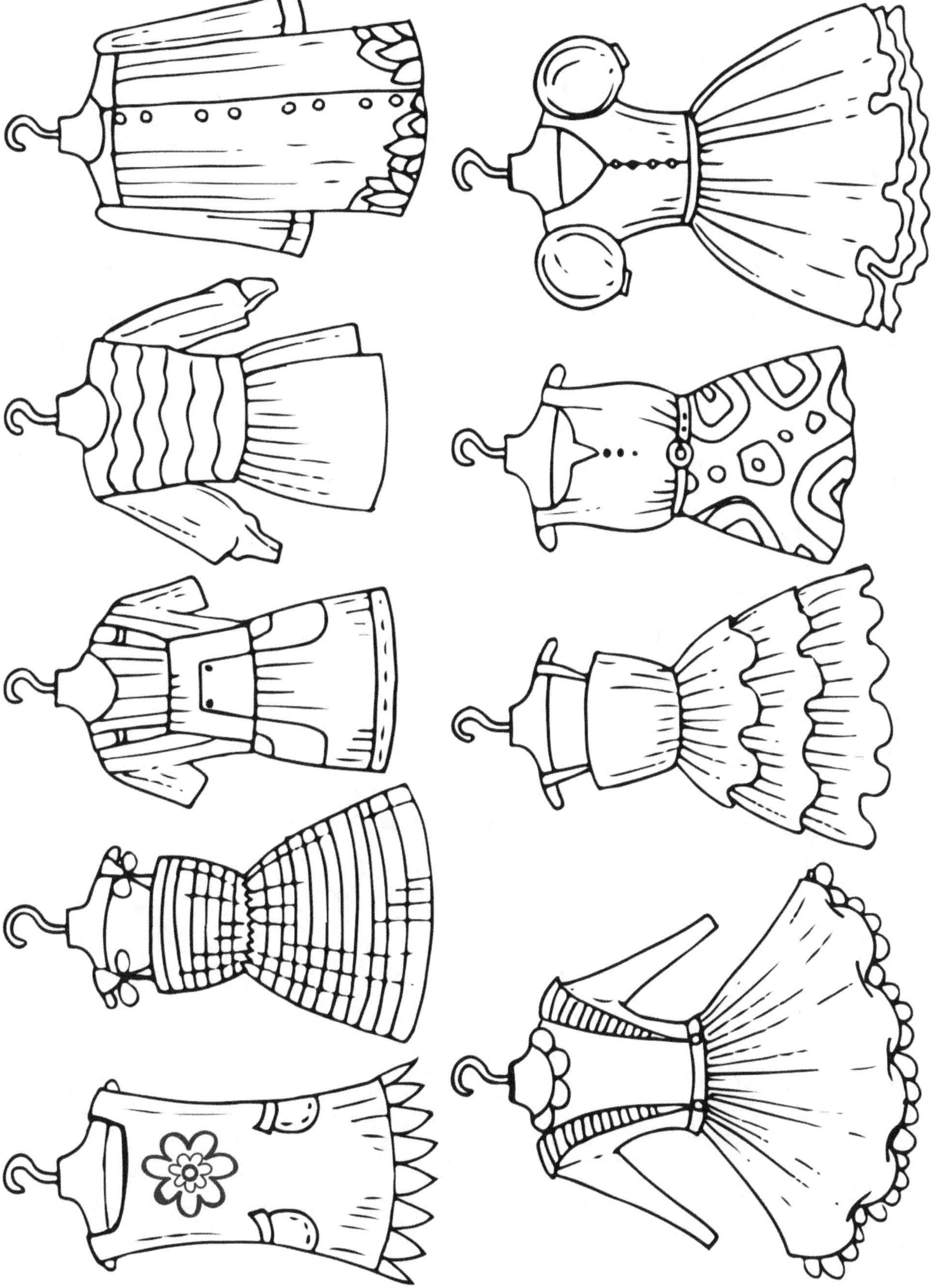

I ♥ DAD
I ♥ MOM
Fashion

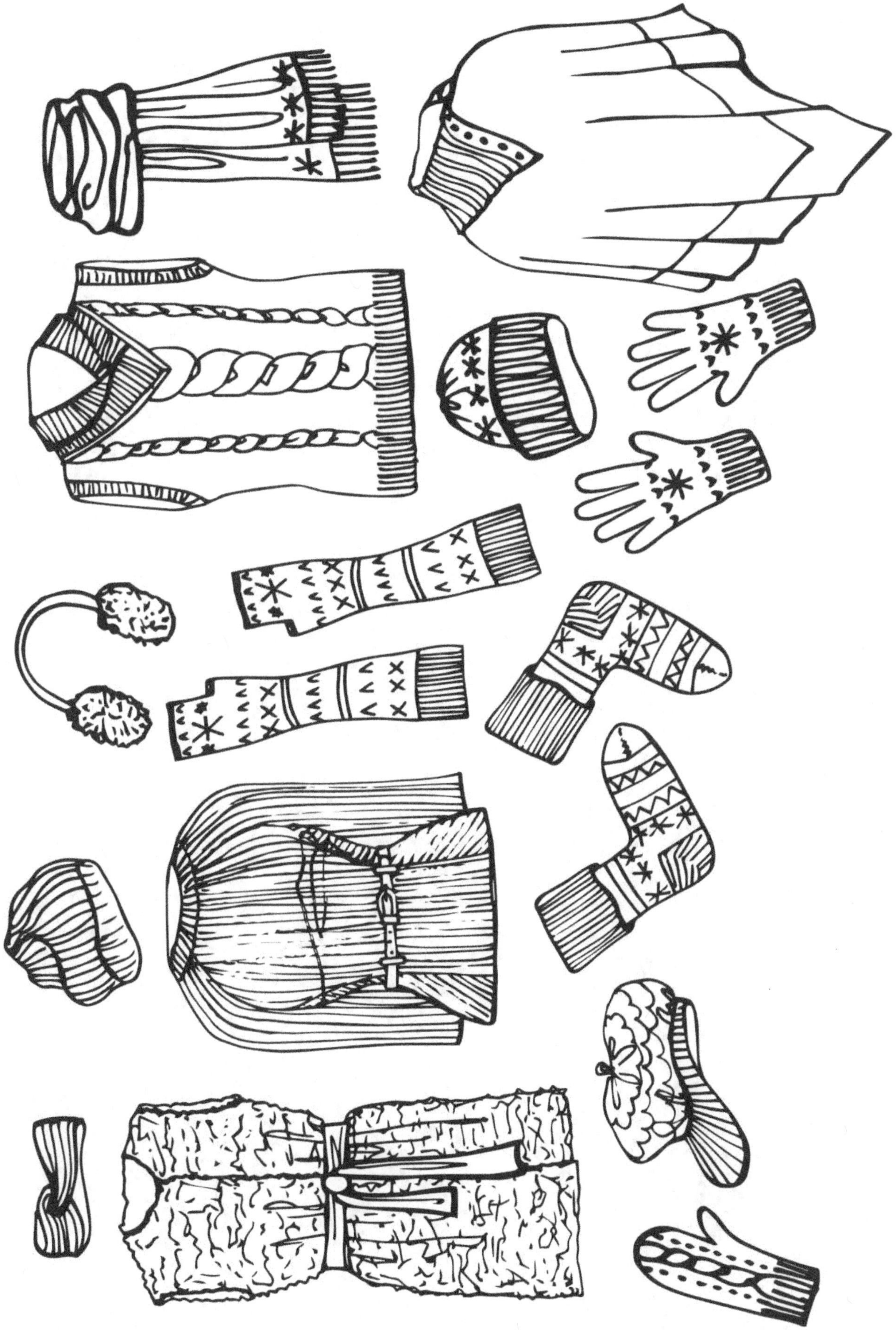

www.ingramcontent.com/pod-product-compliance
Lightning Source LLC
Chambersburg PA
CBHW081423280526
45788CB00009B/3205
* 9 7 8 1 5 4 5 5 8 7 4 6 1 *